M000014699

PADRE PIO

Fabrizio Contessa

PADRE PIO

Venerable — December 18, 1997
Blessed — May 2, 1999
Saint —

ALBA·HOUSE   NEW·YORK

SOCIETY OF ST. PAUL, 2187 VICTORY BLVD., STATEN ISLAND, NEW YORK 10314

ST PAULS

Originally published in Italian by Edizioni San Paolo, s.r.l., under the title *Padre Pio*.

Photo credits:

Casa Sollievo della Sofferenze:
    F. Abresch: cover, pp. 60, 71
    G. Siena: pp. 4, 21, 31, 39, 51, 55
    Edizioni Voce di Padre Pio: p. 64

Library of Congress Cataloging-in-Publication Data

Contessa, Fabrizio, 1966-
    [Padre Pio. English.]
    Padre Pio / Fabrizio Contessa; translated by Edmund C. Lane.
        p. cm.
    ISBN 0-8189-0826-2
    1. Pio, padre, 1887-1968. I. Title.
    BX4705.P49C6613   1999
    271'.3602 — dc21   99-35027
    [B]   CIP

Produced and designed in the United States of America by the Fathers and Brothers of the Society of St. Paul, 2187 Victory Boulevard, Staten Island, New York 10314-6603, as part of their communications apostolate.

ISBN: 0-8189-0826-2

Printing Information:

Current Printing - first digit 1 2 3 4 5 6 7 8 9 10

Year of Current Printing - first year shown

1999   2000   2001   2002   2003   2004   2005   2006

TABLE OF CONTENTS

DEVOTIONS

INTRODUCTION

Christians are profoundly convinced that the Lord in every age does not cease to point out the means necessary to overcome the difficulties in their path. If every age has its evils to torment it, it also has its saints to save it. It was not by chance that the Second Vatican Council energetically invited us to read "the signs of the times." Certainly, God has said everything that needs to be said; he revealed himself fully in his incarnate Son, crucified and risen, but the gift of a saint is in a certain sense a tiny revelation that, in the various circumstances of history, makes the life of the Church easier and more pleasant. "Recalling the saints," St. Bernard of Clairvaux affirms, "stirs in us a desire to enjoy their sweet company."

In the saints, through the power of the Holy Spirit, it is Christ himself who returns to manifest himself on earth. The Lord, obviously, offers the gift of his Spirit for the salvation of all, but in order to be able to "touch" the heart of each one he makes use of some of his children, who more quickly and more clearly allow themselves to be molded by his grace. And they do so to the point of being able to say, along with the apostle Paul: "It is no longer I who live, but Christ who lives in me."

For that reason, in every age the Lord has not failed to console his Church raising up in its midst the saints which it needed. Thus, just to give an example, the age of the great heresies, which threatened the content of the faith itself, had the Fathers of the Church; the crisis of the Twelve Hundreds saw St. Francis of Assisi; the Nineteenth Century positivists were faced with the reality of the supernatural "signs" of Lourdes and St. John Bosco's audacious works of social charity.

In our time, God has sent us, among others, Padre Pio of Pietrelcina, "a saint of modern times," as he was recently defined. In this, naturally, we don't intend to anticipate in any way, the conclusive and official judgment on the sanctity of the Friar of the Stigmata, which belongs to the Church alone in its more authoritative level. If we, then, can only hope to be able one day to venerate Padre Pio as a saint, at the same time we can reasonably remain stupefied at the extraordinary call which, with his life and "miracles," this Beatified Servant of God has offered and continues to offer after his death to the cause of Christ and his Church.

The human unfolding of the life of Padre Pio, so near to us even in time, can therefore well be seen and understood as a "sign of the times" — a fact, a person, a place, some thing that indicates the way to the people of today. To a dynamic age, to an apostolate that makes use of every possible means, to an exaggerated and not rarely sterile activism, Padre Pio has reproposed the choice of "the better part," the one thing necessary. With an echo which, in the last 50 years, has never ceased to resound around the world from the Capuchin convent of San Giovanni Rotondo, a tiny village in the Puglia region of Italy, Padre Pio has shown that in prayer and in the holy sacraments are to be found the only means for obtaining the grace of God necessary in order to obey the commandments and to enjoy, as a pledge already here on this earth, the bliss without end that awaits us in Paradise.

The life of Padre Pio is for these modern times an "open book" from which each one of us can take a lesson in Franciscan humility. In an age in which a certain mentality shows itself proudly fastidious about hearing the word "miracle" pronounced, Padre Pio makes evident the source of our Christian life: the "miracle" of belonging to Jesus Christ and to his Church. The signs of the passion of Jesus impressed on his flesh (the stigmata) and the impressive series of healings obtained through his prayers which are scientifically inexplicable, eloquently point to our human limitations and the power of God. Jesus has told us that "without me you can do nothing."

It is therefore true that, as Pope John Paul II said, "Sanctuaries are essential places, places where one goes to find Grace, even before receiving graces." Multitudes of pilgrims experience this daily when, out of devotion or human curiosity, they approach those places tied to the memory of the Friar of the Stigmata. Theirs is a journey to the rediscovery of that which is essential to faith.

PADRE PIO

HIS LIFE

THE MYSTERY IS MANIFESTED UNEXPECTEDLY

September 20, 1918

It is the morning of September 20, 1918. Europe is by now devastated by the Great War. The "inhuman slaughter" willed by the prevailing political powers and persons with their own interests, both of whom were deaf to the appeals for peace spearheaded by Pope Pius X and then by Benedict XV, was finally coming to an end. A little more than a month later, on November 4th, when the arms are finally laid down the outcome will become horribly apparent. After five years of battle the count will be a good 10 million dead, alongside some 20 million wounded. New armaments and more sophisticated war machinery will have been employed: gas, airplanes, armored tanks, submarines, artillery, machine guns and automatic rifles. The world had witnessed the first scientific annihilation of human beings en masse.

In Italy, which entered the conflict in May of 1915, enthusiasm for the war had given rise to patriotic rhetoric and in the end Italy would count among the dead some 600,00 and among the wounded at least a million. "A useless carnage," was the way the Vicar of Christ defined it.

In 1918 San Giovanni Rotondo was a tiny unknown center of the Gargano promontory (the "spur" on the Italian boot), inhabited by farmers and shepherds. It is located some forty kilometers or twenty-five miles southeast of Foggia on a piece of land, the ancient Daunia, which for centuries had been trodden by pilgrims on their way to the Sanctuary of Monte Sant'Angelo. But the town is nonetheless isolated from other nearby localities because the only road which leads there is made up of an infinite series of curves carved out of the rock.

So, on the morning of September 20, 1918, a Friday, in this lost village of poor folks who lacked electric lights, running water and a sewage system, an extraordinary fact took place whose echo was destined to reach beyond the confines itself of Europe, whose Christian image had been so disfigured by the inhuman bloodbath of the Great War.

Nothing, on that morning, would lead one to guess what was about to happen. In the ancient convent of the Capuchins everything seemed tranquil. A young religious, Padre Pio, had just finished saying Mass in the little church dedicated to the Madonna delle Grazie and had retired alone to the choir where he used to make his thanksgiving before a large crucifix. His prayer that day was more intense than usual, however, culminating in ecstasy. Suddenly, from the crucifix five rays of light came forth wounding the hands, feet and side of that young friar. They were the stigmata, signs of the passion of Christ, which from that moment on would accompany Padre Pio until the end of his earthly existence.

Here is how Padre Pio himself described the event in a letter to his spiritual director: "I was in the choir after the celebration of Holy Mass when sleep overtook me by surprise, like a sweet dream. All my senses, internal and external, as well as the very faculties of my soul, found themselves wrapped in an indescribable peace (…). And while all this was going on I saw myself before a mysterious figure: his hands, feet and side were dripping with blood. His look was frightening."

"What I felt in that instant," Padre Pio's narrative continues, "I don't know how to describe. I felt I was dying, and I would be dead if the Lord had not intervened to bolster the heart which I felt pounding in my chest. The sight of the figure faded and I saw that my hands, feet and side had been pierced and were dripping blood!"

In reality, the stigmata had already made its first appearance in 1910 but Padre Pio had asked the Lord that it might go away and he was granted this grace. But from that morning in 1918 the stigmata would accompany him for the next 50 years. The names of Padre Pio and San Giovanni Rotondo would become ever more famous and would be indissolubly linked, so much so that today, more than thirty years after his death, millions of people each year come on pilgrimage to the tomb of this humble Friar, the protagonist of such prodigious facts and events that science and human reason alone cannot explain them, but which the faith of the Christian people recognize as "miracles."

Are we talking about a saint? Many would say yes. The Church, with the prudence and wisdom of the ages, has not yet said so officially though it seems close to doing so. Pope John Paul II, in his visit to San Giovanni Rotondo in 1983, went out of his way to stop at the tomb of Padre Pio of Pietrelcina where he spent some time in prayer. Such a gesture gave many reason to hope. This was followed shortly thereafter by a formal declaration of the heroic virtues of this Servant of God. Then came the promulgation on December 21, 1988 of a miracle attributed to his intercession. His beatification on May 2, 1999 in St. Peter's Square before an overflow crowd of well over 200,000 with an additional 100,000 present before a gigantic screen in the Square of St. John Lateran, was the next to the last step leading to what many hope will be his eventual canonization.

His infancy and prophetic vision

The earthly sojourn of Padre Pio, in the world known as Francesco Forgione, began in Pietrelcina, a rough and rocky village in the Sannio region (Pietrelcina means "Little Rock") some thirteen kilometers or eight miles from Benevento. The fourth of seven brothers, Francesco was born on May 25, 1887 to Orazio (also called "Razio" or "zi'Razio"), his father, and Peppa, his mother. The family, as most families in those days, was very poor, so much so that his father was forced twice to emigrate to America. Francesco was educated in the faith and traditional values of Italy at that time. Thus when his father wanted to kiss the hands of his celebrated son — after he had received the stigmata — he would hear his son say: "Never! A son must kiss the hands of his parents, and not the parents those of their son."

Francesco's childhood was spent in the silence of the home where his mother frequently left him alone in order to go and work in the fields. He often played with his brothers and friends, but when he heard someone using bad language he would shut himself in the house. "I would rather die or at least become deaf," he would say, "rather than hear the kinds of insults which men address to God... and most of all with those horrendous blasphemies."

From the time he was very small, it seems, he showed a desire to dedicate himself entirely to the service of God. Very early the apparitions and ecstasies began. Luigi Peroni, the biographer of Padre Pio, recalls: "The devil made himself known, forcing himself on the little child, who was barely five years old, with all his infernal rage. He appeared to him dressed as a man or a beast under an 'obscene form' often presenting himself in the guise of persons dear to him." In that same period, his confessor Padre Agostino will recall, the thought and desire to consecrate himself for ever to the Lord occurred to him for the first time.

But it was when he was fifteen, in 1902, that Francesco had the imposing and upsetting vision that would in some way indicate the direction of his life. Telling about it to a confrere, Francesco spoke of two groups of men, one with "beautiful faces and dressed in white," the others with "a frightening aspect" and "dressed in black." Francesco's soul, in the middle of the two groups, is called to fight a giant, "a man of such immeasurable height that his head touched the clouds." A radiant figure who was at his side urged him to do so: "I will be right here: I will help you and will not let him hurt you." The encounter was fierce but Francesco got the upper hand and won. The radiant figure was about to place a crown on his head, but then withdrew it saying: "Another crown more beautiful yet I have reserved for you if you know how to do battle with the one with whom you have just fought. He will return, always on the attack. Fight him valiantly and never doubt my help." It is the battle with the devil which will be repeated countless times in the course of his existence.

Like Friar Camillo

The yoke of the Lord is easy. Notwithstanding all the tests, torments and sufferings which one can encounter on the way, the way of the Lord is simple. Like a child who casts his glance on the world, the life of faith grows through curiosity and desire. "What else can one love if not those things which are beautiful?" Saint Augustine asks.

By the time he had the vision of the "great battle," the desire to become a Capuchin had already grown in the youthful Francesco. The Christian life, even that of the great mystics, is always marked by encounters and events which are entirely human, by means of which the Lord intends to ground us in reality. Thus Francesco remained fascinated by the figure of Friar Camillo, the young mendicant friar from the nearby monastery of Morcone, who from time to time would arrive at Pietrelcina all covered with dust. Friar Camillo would refresh himself at the village fountain, tell stories about Saint Francis to the children, and make the rounds of the houses to ask for a little bread as alms for the love of God.

The smiling face of this friar and his imposing long black beard excited the children's fantasy. Francesco certainly did not know who the Capuchins were, but he wanted to become "like Friar Camillo." He himself will recount: "Friar Camillo's beard was fixed in my head and no one could get it out."

So, at the age of fifteen, in the Spring of 1902, Francesco asked the Capuchins for permission to enter the novitiate in Morcone, where he would make his entrance on January 6th of the following year. The one to accept Francesco in the monastery would be Friar Camillo himself. Thus the doors to religious life and the vows of poverty, obedience and chastity, which Francesco would solemnly profess on January 27, 1907, were opened to him. According to an ancient custom, his name was also changed. The Superior gave him the name Pio, followed by that of the locality from which he came. Francesco Forgione would become Pio of Pietrelcina.

The Arrival at San Giovanni Rotondo

On July 28, 1916, Friar Pio for the first time left for San Giovanni Rotondo in the province of Foggia. Here the Capuchins had, some two kilometers (about a mile) outside the place, a half-ruined monastery. The people would go there to venerate the image of Santa Maria delle Grazie. And it was there, except for brief interruptions, that Padre Pio would remain for fifty-two years until his death.

San Giovanni Rotondo constituted for him a destination in an itinerary already marked, notwithstanding his young age, by thousands of trials and tribulations. Friar Pio's constitution had for some years begun to show evident and strange symptoms of fatigue, sudden facial flushes and impressive pallor. Religious life was difficult and Friar Pio made it harder still. He undertook more fasts than those prescribed and punished himself with vigils and flagellations that went beyond the rule. His food diminished both qualitatively and quantitatively. "My stomach can only hold a little water," he would say to his spiritual director; only the community spirit would make him sit with his confreres in the refectory at mealtimes. One night, in July of 1907, weak cries could be heard coming from his cell in the monastery. A brother, frightened, ran to his side to find him lying on the floor with a haggard look and labored breathing.

The constitution of this young friar did not respond in the end to the solicitude of his brothers to the point that they began to seriously fear for his life. Friar Pio therefore asked the ultimate favor: to become a priest and to celebrate Mass at least once. His request would be granted. Anticipating by ten months with respect to the time prescribed back then by Canon Law (one had to be at least twenty-four years old), he was ordained a priest on August 10, 1910 in the cathedral of Benevento.

Padre Pio would not die but neither would his suffering cease. His health continued to be precarious and for that reason, except for brief periods in which he would return to the monastery, the superiors preferred to station him in his own hometown, Pietrelcina, where depending on his strength he would help the parish priest. He would leave Pietrelcina for the call to arms in November of 1915 (registration number 2094/25), but illness forced him to continual sick leaves during which he would spend time in various monasteries, among them San Giovanni Rotondo.

Some time after his ordination, the first signs of the passion of the Lord appeared on his body. Frightened, as he himself confessed, the young Capuchin priest "prayed to the Lord that he might have such a visible phenomenon taken away." The Lord heard him. However, even when the visible signs of the wounds were not present, the pain was always there which made itself felt "in certain circumstances and on specific days," especially on Wednesday and from Thursday evening until Saturday. It is the period of the so-called "invisible" stigmata. For him too, even if in a very special way, the logic of the Gospel held true: one does not enter into glory without passing by the way of sorrow and the passion.

STIGMATIZED

The same anguish as that of Christ

"O my Father, I am dying of sorrow for the mortification and ensuing confusion which I experience in the most intimate part of my soul. I fear that I shall die from loss of blood if the Lord does not heed the cries of my poor heart, and take this affliction from me... Will Jesus, who is so good, grant me this grace? Will he at least take from me this confusion which I feel over these signs? I raise my voice to him with all my strength and I will not stop supplicating him until, in his mercy he takes from me not the agony or the pain... because I see this to be impossible... but these external signs which cause me such indescribable and unbearable humiliation." These words of Padre Pio are full of anguish and at the same time they have a familiar ring. Only a month has passed from that September 20th of 1918, the day on which he received "visibly" the stigmata of the passion and, still upset over what has happened, Padre Pio thus turns to his own spiritual Father.

The words are familiar: "I am afraid of bleeding to death if the Lord does not hear the cries of my poor heart." "Will Jesus, who is so good, grant me this grace?" Upon hearing these words every Christian will immediately recall the crucial and dramatic passages of the passion of Jesus Christ, as in the Garden of Olives: "Father, if it is your will, take this cup from me, yet not my will, but yours be done" (Lk 22:42), or like the last tortured cry from the cross: "My God, my God, why have you forsaken me?" (Mk 15:34).

The anguished cry of Padre Pio, more than one has said, are the words of a saint. There exists, in fact, in Christian events a realism which is a thousand miles from fanaticism and which always takes into just account every factor, every element of the human experience. Thus even suffering, even though Christianly supported with the help of God, does not cease to be such. While knowing its salvific value, faced with sorrow the Christian — following the example of Jesus himself — asks simply and humanly that "the cup" be taken away. For this reason the Christians of the first few centuries, while in the context of unheard-of persecutions, considered the ambition to be glorified as a martyr a grave sin of pride, a challenge to God, and the most subtle of temptations. Even in this Padre Pio was like his Master who, in the desert responded to the temptations of the devil citing the ancient writings of his people: "It is written: You will not tempt the Lord your God" (Mt 4:7).

The signs of Jesus

Padre Pio received the visible stigmata on Friday, the morning of September 20, 1918, after having said Mass and while he was making his usual thanksgiving before a huge crucifix. The moment he saw blood dripping, overcome with fright, he dashed from the choir where he had been in prayer and rushed to his cell. Here he sought to stop the flow of blood with cloths and handkerchiefs.

Padre Pio was alone that day in the monastery. The other two religious were in town doing some shopping, and the fifteen young men who were guests of the little seminary were playing in the courtyard after breakfast. Padre Paolino, returning to the monastery, noted his staggering and irregular gait and the bandages that Padre Pio, in his shame, sought to hide under the ample folds of his habit. He accompanied him to his cell and wanted to know what had happened. Extremely upset,

Padre Paolino wrote to his Provincial Superior, who, while waiting for a chance to see with his own eyes, gave but one order: say nothing to anyone.

Having gone to San Giovanni Rotondo, the Provincial Superior was able to personally acquaint himself with the details surrounding this extraordinary event. He saw, and wrote thus to the Superior General of the Capuchins: "They are not blemishes or imprints but true wounds perforating the hands and feet. The one on the side is a real gash which continuously oozes blood or a bloody liquid." The Superior General will likewise display prudence and the greatest discretion.

For Padre Pio this will be the beginning of another "calvary," that of countless visits to doctors by whom he was subjected to all kinds of tests to verify the nature of these wounds. "My God! What confusion and humiliation," Padre Pio would write, "in having to manifest what You have done in this miserable creature!"

Professor Luigi Romanelli examined Padre Pio for two days almost without interruption and in the end would testify: "I am convinced, indeed I am sure, that these wounds are not superficial, because applying the thumb to the palm of his hand and the index finger on the back and applying pressure one has the precise sensation of an existing void. On his side I observed a clean cut, parallel to the ribs, seven or eight centimeters (a little over three inches) long, with an excision of the softer tissue."

It is in this context that an abrupt encounter with Padre Agostino Gemelli, physician and psychologist and one of the most esteemed Italian religious personalities who in those years had begun to work on the foundation of Milan's Catholic University, also took place. Father Gemelli arrived at the monastery of San Giovanni Rotondo on April 18, 1920 in order to be able to examine Padre Pio's wounds. In the meantime the Holy See, through the Congregation that then bore the name of the Holy Office, had established that no one could examine his wounds without written authorization. Padre Gemelli probably thought that an exception could be made for him and insisted that he might be shown the wounds. Padre Pio, however, obeying the order of the Vatican, very firmly refused, insisting that he had not been authorized to do so.

The matter created quite an uproar, also because some years later Padre Gemelli in a long article in the magazine *Vita e Pensiero*, while not naming Padre Pio, judged all stigmatists in the history of the Church, with the possible exception of St. Francis of Assisi, to be "possible hysterics, endowed with a very poor spirituality." To Padre Gemelli the authoritative *Civiltà Cattolica* promptly replied saying that those "possible hysterics of very poor spirituality" had been declared saints by the Church, while precisely in those days another stigmatist, Gemma Galgani, was about to be declared Blessed.

The Stigmata

The phenomenon — More than three hundred: so many are the stigmatists — excluding those discovered to be pathological or self-inflicted — of whom we have historical evidence and who have been examined scientifically. Of these some seventy whose stigmata have been held to be true, that is, manifested spontaneously, "without material cause," have been elevated by the Church to the honor of the altars. Italy, France, Spain, Belgium and Peru are the countries principally involved in this phenomenon. Religious are more numerous than lay persons. Padre Pio is the first priest (St. Francis of Assisi, the most famous of the canonized stigmatists, was not a priest but a deacon) and he lived with the signs of the passion of Jesus for 50 years, far longer than any other. St. Francis had the stigmata for two years, St. Gemma Galgani for eighteen months.

The case of Padre Pio — The friar of Pietrelcina received the stigmata on September 20, 1918. The "lacerations" of the tissue did not result from external agents or other pathology, appeared unexpectedly and were accompanied by hemorrhages and terrible pain. The wounds, round in shape "almost circular, with clean edges and a diameter of a little more than two centimeters [three-quarters of an inch]," never in fifty years were subject to infection, decomposition, infiltration, edema, or inflammation; instead they remained stationary, unchanging, not tending to heal, not becoming gangrenous, not emitting a foul odor, but rather, according to countless witnesses, giving off a floral perfume. The stigmata disappeared the day preceding the death of Padre Pio without leaving a sign or scar in the area which they uninterruptedly occupied for 18,261 days.

Medical examinations — Three doctors were assigned to visit Padre Pio: Doctor Luigi Romanelli, chief of the Hospital of Barletta who visited him at the request of the Provincial Curia of the Capuchins; Doctor Luigi Festa, in charge of the General Curia of the same Order; Professor Antonio Bignami, head of Pathological Medicine at the University of Rome who received his assignment directly from the Holy See. Romanelli and Festa presented their findings which, after an attentive and meticulous examination, resulted in their conclusion that "the wounds of Padre Pio are not in fact classifiable, by their character and by their clinical history, among common surgical lesions" (Romanelli) and that from the examination of Padre Pio's members "there emerges a series of interesting phenomena, harmoniously linked together, which are outside the control of objective inquiry and which the science we possess, as vast and profound as it is, is not able to explain." The wounds, for the first two doctors, are hence of a nature unknown to medical science.

It was not thus, at least initially and at least in part, for the third doctor. For Professor Bignami, illustrious clinician and declared atheist, the wounds were "perhaps" in part of morbid origin and in part artificially provoked. That is they "began as a pathological product and, then, perhaps unconsciously and through the phenomenon of auto-suggestion, they assumed their symmetry and were maintained artificially through chemical means, for example with tincture of iodine." This hypothesis did not stand the "test of fire." Since Professor Bignami held that Padre Pio alone caused the wounds, he made him wear some special sealed bandages for eight consecutive days. The wounds ought to have healed. On the eighth day, instead, when the seals were removed the wounds were still open and bleeding profusely.

Miracles

"Ask and you shall receive"

"Padre Pio, the Saint of San Giovanni Rotondo has performed a miracle on the person of the registrar of the town." With this six-column headline published in the daily newspaper *Il Mattino* on June 20, 1919 and the clamor surrounding the "phenomenon," Padre Pio left the confines of the little town of the Gargano for the first time. While doctors minutely examined the bloody and marginless lesions carved into the body of Padre Pio, news of the stigmata and of the miracles performed by the friar of Pietrelcina, notwithstanding the official reserve, spread rapidly even reaching the newspapers. And so began the unstoppable flow of pilgrims to San Giovanni Rotondo which will make of this forgotten village in the center of Puglia one of the most visited cities in all of Italy.

At first those who come are driven by curiosity alone. Later they are moved also by devotion. They come from every part of the world and belong to every social class. There are believers and unbelievers. There are those who think that the stigmata is just a trick to attract the naive and unsuspecting pilgrims, but there are also those who come to San Giovanni Rotondo as unbelievers and who leave convinced. The simple people, who are

not blinded by the stubborn and dire rationalism of the learned, bring along with them, together with the heavy burden of the preoccupations, anxieties and dramas with which their daily lives are often shackled, hope in an "extraordinary" gesture of mercy from the Lord. Anchored in the Christian tradition, the people know that if one prays with faith the Lord grants miracles. It is reasonable to hope in this way because for God who is omnipotent all things are possible. It is reasonable to pray in this way because Jesus himself was the one to suggest it: "Ask and you shall receive" (Mt 7:7). For this reason to those who had the nerve to inquire of him, "Do you perform miracles?" Padre Pio would simply respond: "I am only a friar who prays."

Extraordinary signs

Many, indeed very many, are the miracles of Padre Pio, or better, miracles performed by the Lord which the faithful have attributed to the prayer and intercession of this holy friar. It is obviously impossible to recall all of them. For the sake of brevity, we will mention two stories, perhaps among the most familiar, but also among the most moving and significant.

The blind girl who regained her sight — Gemma De Giorgi, who was born in 1939, was blind from birth. As an infant, her parents very quickly became aware that something was not right with her eyes and they subjected her to numerous visits to specialists hoping that something could be done. Well-known oculists concluded, however, that the infant was born without pupils and hence would never be able to see. When she was six and a half years old, it came time for her to make her first communion. Her grandmother thought of taking the little one to San Giovanni Rotondo where, she knew, there was a friar who performed miracles. The little girl was encouraged to ask the priest to intercede for her healing, but she forgot to do so. Padre Pio, however, during her confession, had placed his hands on her eyes, tracing the sign of the cross. At communion time, he once again made the sign of the cross on Gemma's eyes. During the trip home, the child said to her grandmother that she could see clearly. Doctors confirmed the fact that she could see even though in their unanimous opinion it was impossible because one cannot see without pupils.

A mother healed of cancer — It is November 1962. Professor Wanda Poltawska, actively involved in the Polish diocese of Krakow, is dying of cancer of the throat and doctors no longer offer her any hope. The news spread rapidly eventually reaching Rome where the Capitular Vicar of Krakow was attending the celebration of the Second Vatican Council. His name was Bishop Karol Wojtyla, the future Pope John Paul II. Bishop Wojtyla had known the family of Professor Poltawska for a long time and was profoundly struck by the sad news which reached him from his far off homeland. So, on November 17 a letter mailed from Rome and written in Latin was addressed to the "famous" friar of the stigmata whom Bishop Wojtyla had been able to meet several years earlier when, as a young priest, he went to confession in San Giovanni Rotondo. Thus wrote the future pope: "Venerable Padre, I ask you to pray for a mother of four young girls who is forty years old and lives in Krakow, Poland. During the last war she spent five years in a concentration camp in Germany and now finds herself in very great danger to her health and indeed to her life, on account of cancer. Pray that God, through the intervention of the Blessed Virgin, might show mercy to her and to her family." On November 28, eleven days later, another letter reached Padre Pio from the Polish bishop: "Venerable Padre, the woman who lives in Krakow, Poland, mother of four young girls, on November 21, as she was about to undergo surgery, was suddenly cured. Thanking God and also you, venerable Padre, I offer my most heartfelt gratitude in the name of this woman, her husband and all her family."

His many charisms

"He who believes in me will do the works I do and greater far than these" (Jn 14:12). Observing the extraordinary charisms of Padre Pio, gifts granted by the Lord to remind us of his merciful presence in history, how can our minds fail to recall these enigmatic and prophetic words of Jesus? If the stigmata are the best known "signs" associated with the passion of Christ, and healing miracles "signs" which visibly point to the mercy of the Lord, in Padre Pio there were also other gifts, other powers which place him on the same level as that of the most extraordinary saints which the tradition of the Church can enumerate.

Bilocation, perfumes, hypothermia (high fever reaching 48 degrees Celsius; 118 degrees Fahrenheit), prophecies, healings, the ability to read hearts, the ability to sustain prolonged vigils and fasts beyond all human power to endure recapitulated in Padre Pio the prodigious works which took place in the lives of St. Francis of Assisi, St. Anthony of Padua, St. Teresa of Jesus, and St. Joseph of Cupertino. Millions are the faithful who, approaching Padre Pio, were able to receive spiritual as well as material benefits through these gifts. Pope Benedict XV when he learned of such a flowering of charisms said: "Truly Padre Pio is one of those extraordinary men whom God from time to time sends on earth to convert hearts."

Perfume — Would a friar of known sanctity be so vain as to douse himself with so much perfume? Yes, Padre Pio was even accused of this; it happened that someone, not aware of this particular gift, was scandalized. Padre Pio, in fact, gave off a particular perfume which some have compared to that of violets and others to a mixture of rose and cyclamen. For those who had the fortune to notice it, this perfume reached the faithful who were closest to the friar. But not only. The perfume could be noted on the objects which he touched, on the clothing he wore, in the places where he passed. Moreover, that perfume, which believers call the odor of sanctity, was noticeable even at a distance, like a passing breeze, to indicate a particular spiritual presence of Padre Pio. Many insist on having perceived it more than once after his death.

Authoritative witness to this particular odor of Padre Pio, which being more penetrating has nothing whatsoever to do with normal perfume, was Professor Luigi Romanelli who in a report wrote the following: "In June of 1919, when I arrived for the first time at San Giovanni Rotondo, as soon as I was introduced to Padre Pio, I noticed that a certain odor came from his person, so much so that it seemed to me that it wasn't a very good thing that a friar, in the then held concept, would use perfume. Mine was not suggestion, because no one had ever spoken to me about such a phenomenon."

A yet more surprising testimony was raised by Doctor Giorgio Festa because he himself was "in fact lacking all sense of smell." For Doctor Festa the perfume, more than from the person, was coming from the blood of Padre Pio. It was a "pleasant perfume, almost a mixture of violets and roses. One considers that among the tissues of the human organism," the Doctor noted, "blood is that which decomposes most rapidly. In any case it never lets off a pleasant odor."

Bilocation — such a phenomenon consists in finding oneself in different places at the same time, in one place with one's body, in another with one's spirit clothed in a bodily form. Well-known is the bilocation of Padre Pio who, while remaining in his monastery, was found at the same time at the side of the Supreme Commandant of the Italian Armed Forces, General Luigi Cadorna, who was contemplating suicide after the catastrophic defeat at Caporetto. The friar appeared in the office of the Commandant and convinced him to put his pistol away. When the General, who had never seen Padre Pio, visited the monastery of San Giovanni Rotondo he at once recognized him as the friar who had saved his life. And one can well imagine the surprise of the high military officer when Padre Pio greeted him with the words, "General, that was a nasty night we spent together!"

Reading consciences — By means of another

particular divine gift it seems that Padre Pio could read the secrets of the soul like an open book. Almost always in the confessional, but also on other occasions, he seemed to know already in advance what one ought to say or even more what one intended to keep hidden. Countless are the testimonies in this regard. Famous is the one regarding Cesare Festa, a Masonic lawyer and cousin of Doctor Giorgio Festa. After lengthy discussions with his cousin, Cesare allowed himself to be convinced into going to San Giovanni Rotondo. "If you are an honest man," Giorgio had told him, "you will go and see for yourself with your own eyes." And so Cesare went. When he arrived at the monastery Padre Pio was surrounded by a group of people. Padre Pio left the others and, while not knowing who he was, went up to meet him. "How is it that you are here?" Padre Pio asked. "Aren't you a Mason?" With loyalty, the lawyer answered, "Yes, Padre." "And what is your job in the Masons?" "To fight the Church from the political point of view." After some moments of silence, with an unforeseeable gesture, Padre Pio took him by the hand as if he were a little boy and told him the parable of the Prodigal Son. An hour later the celebrated Masonic lawyer went to confession and received the pardon of God. Later on, having been persecuted by the Masons, Cesare Festa became a Third Order Franciscan.

Prophecy — Padre Pio also had this particular gift by means of which some privileged souls are able to predict future events or things. The Friar of Pietrelcina always made use of it for the good of souls. Among the many possible episodes, the one that comes to mind is the one in which he predicted the pontificate of Paul VI. Some years before Cardinal Montini was elected pope, Alberto Galletti, a Commander from Milan, asked Padre Pio for a blessing for his archbishop who — you guessed it — was Cardinal Montini. "Not a blessing, but a flood!" Padre Pio answered, "and my unworthy prayer. But you tell the Archbishop that, after this one, he will be the pope. Do you understand? You must tell him, because he has to prepare himself."

ALTAR AND CONFESSIONAL

The two poles of the priesthood

"As a religious he generously lived out the ideal of the Capuchin friars, just as he lived out the ideal of the priesthood." It is the afternoon of Saturday May 23, 1987, and with these brief words Pope John Paul II, in a pastoral visit to San Giovanni Rotondo, delineated the figure of Padre Pio. Karol Wojtyla, before ascending the throne of Peter, had twice (in 1947 and in 1962) had the opportunity of personally meeting the friar of the stigmata and was impressed. Speaking now as Pope just a few feet from his tomb, he did not spend any time on the many extraordinary "signs" or on the countless miracles that had accompanied the life of Padre Pio.

The particular gifts, the special charisms that God occasionally concedes to those among his children whom he wishes, are never something private, a possession to be enjoyed for one's own enrichment or even simply for one's own personal sanctity. Charisms, and among these the stigmata and the other miracles performed by Padre Pio, are given for the good of all, for the edification of the Church. They are only potent and exceptional "signs" to remind us, that bring us back to Another, just like street signs that indicate to us the direction of the road.

Pope John Paul II, who doesn't in any way undervalue the importance of miracles, knows well however that the first "healing" is to be in the grace of God. The other graces, even the most precious, do not in themselves save, they don't take away sin, they are not permanently connected with the Christian's state of holiness. Sanctifying grace which one receives at baptism, on the other hand, is. Sanctifying grace is the most important gift because it makes us sharers in the very life of God himself. It is this same grace which, lost even a thousand times in one's life through sin, is reacquired by seriously going to confession and nourishing oneself with the Eucharist. The authority of

Padre Pio, in the end, lies precisely in this, in having reminded us, by means of these exceptional charisms, of what is essential in the Christian life.

"Were not the altar and the confessional the two poles of his life?" John Paul II asked on his visit to the sanctuary of San Giovanni Rotondo. "Even today he offers a point of reference," Pope Wojtyla underscored, "insofar as in him are to be found with a particular welcome and spiritual resonance two aspects that characterize the Catholic priesthood: the faculty of consecrating the Body and Blood of the Lord and that of remitting sins."

The words of Pope John Paul II seem to echo those uttered some years earlier by another great pope, Paul VI, who confronted with the whole world's rush to see Padre Pio, asked himself: "Look at what fame he had! What worldwide clientele he gathered about himself. But why? Perhaps because he was a philosopher, because he was a wise man, because he had means at his disposition?" And he offered this succinct reply: "Because he said Mass humbly, heard confessions from dawn to dusk… and bore the wounds of our Lord."

For half a century, from 1918 to 1968, one watched the stigmatized Capuchin of San Giovanni Rotondo. To attract what Pope Paul VI called "a worldwide clientele" were his inexplicable stigmata. But those who went up to the monastery of Santa Maria delle Grazie were never able to see the stigmata which Padre Pio kept jealously hidden. All the same one could see and meet that priest who so painfully resembled Jesus Christ.

Padre Pio's day

Fifteen, sixteen, at times even nineteen hours a day he spent between the altar and the confessional. The work undertaken by Padre Pio was truly admirable. Little by little as the fame of this stigmatized friar spread, a veritable and uncontainable river of humanity flowed into San Giovanni Rotondo. So much so that, to put some discipline into the press of the crowd wanting to go to confession to him, it was found necessary to open an office where one could sign up and take a ticket indicating the order of ingress. Each one had to wait his or her turn, whether Italian or foreigner, priest or lay person, celebrity or ordinary individual. There were those who had to wait ten or even as many as fifteen days, sleeping on the bare earth surrounding the monastery. Sometimes, on account of the great influx of penitents, the intervention of the police was made indispensable.

Padre Pio's "work day" began very early. He got up at 3:30 while all the others in the monastery were still sleeping. He went down to the little church to prepare himself in prayer for his Mass which began at 5:00. The predawn hour had been willed by Padre Pio himself in order to give the possibility to the farmers — or to the "cafoni" as he called them and as he defined himself — to assist at Mass before going into the fields. But his Mass was not attended only by farmers. Many pilgrims came up from the city as early as midnight to take their places behind the single door giving access to the little church. Whether it was raining or snowing or whether the wind was blowing violently down Monte Nero whirling and whistling on its way, these people stood there huddled together in groups, ready to be the first to go in. It is estimated that all together twenty million people have been present at a Mass celebrated by Padre Pio.

Padre Pio's Mass was always memorable. No one who ever attended one remained unmoved. And it was not a matter of actively participating or of doing something. "Silence and kneeling": how many times Padre Pio recommended this comportment to those who surrounded his altar. And the faithful, attentive and devout, followed the very long rite with attention: the moment of the elevation when the bread and wine truly become the body and blood of Christ, could last more than fifteen minutes. Jesus crucified and Padre Pio stigmatized assumed an impressive oneness on the altar. Padre Pio received in his own flesh the pain, the sacrifice of Jesus. "Padre Pio's Mass," one witness records, "is different from all the other Masses that are celebrated in this world, not for any diversity in the liturgical rite, not for a different interpretation, but because he renews the passion of the Nazarene, becoming himself a living Host." A priest who saw him celebrate confessed: "From the time I attended a Mass of Padre Pio, I have never been able to thoughtlessly rush through my Mass."

The crucified friar of the Gargano, in the end, went up to the altar as to his own Calvary, to gather the treasures of the redemption which he then distributed to each one in the confessional. And in fact, once the Mass was over, except for a brief pause for a bite to eat and personal prayer, Padre Pio dedicated himself totally to the souls of sinners. It is estimated that five million people approached his confessional over the years. Confession to him was rapid and to the point, averaging three minutes. He wanted to hear only the essentials. And he heard about twenty persons an hour, sixty women and sixty men between morning and afternoon.

Still he never heard a confession on the run. Even the administration of the sacrament of Penance meant suffering for Padre Pio. That is why he has also been justly called the "Martyr of the Confessional." He suffered in his own flesh for the sins committed against the Lord: "Pray that you not be cast out," he said to a confrere before entering the confessional. "If you knew," he once said to a priest, "how tremendous it is to sit in the tribunal of the confessional! We administer the blood of Christ. We have to be careful not to disperse it easily and without care."

For this reason Padre Pio wanted one's confession to be brief, clear, integral and sincere. He could not support hesitation, facile justifications or, worse, insincerity. He is there and it seems that with his eyes he can scrutinize the hearts and consciences of the penitents. When a certain sin refuses to come out, he would interrupt. "Beh! Now tell me… Did you ever…?" The penitent stutters, turns pale. Sometimes the confession is completed, sometimes the penitent is sent away: "Go away and don't come back until.…" The tone of his voice could be severe and harsh. And still these are the souls that he loved the most. For the average priest it would be a mistake with grave consequences to want to imitate the comportment of Padre Pio in the confessional, because his methods are not the result of a particular tactic or of some calculation, but only the consequence of the possession of a knowledge which goes beyond the limits of human possibility. Illumined by the Holy Spirit he knows that these expulsions are the salutary hand of the Lord that will shake those souls up. A penitent attacked by Padre Pio only after repeated attempts, admits: "Until now no one had ever truly shook me up, and so it was easy for me to justify myself in my errors.…"

What most surprises us however was the fact that those who were bruskly thrown out didn't leave San Giovanni Rotondo. They wandered about the surrounding countryside, even for days, with eyes downcast. At times they wept. They always returned to the confessional and sincerely sought God's forgiveness and the strength to change. For Padre Pio this was his greatest joy! He said: "I can punish my children, but woe to anyone else who touches them." In fact, one reads in Scripture: "Those whom I love, I reprove and chastise" (Rv 3:19).

A SON OF HOLY OBEDIENCE

Years of Testing

The entire life of Padre Pio up to this point was marked by charisms such as to define him as the greatest wonder worker of the century. Together with the five wounds which remained open and bleeding for fifty years, other gifts contributed to making his figure truly outside the common norm of people: the instantaneous healings performed or foretold by him; the ability to read thoughts and predict the future; the ecstasies and visions of Christ, the Virgin Mary and the saints; his battles, at times even physical, with the devil; the mysterious perfume which emanated from his person; the high fevers. He had to defend himself, sometimes bruskly and sharply from the imaginable curiosity and fanaticism of the mobs. He did not defend himself, instead, from the hostility of some ecclesiastics, even when it seemed evident that their comportment was not dictated exclusively by the prudence due when confronted by a "phenomenon" so extraordinary and mysterious.

The most acute suffering — as is not infrequent with the saints — he had in fact to suffer precisely from some men of the Church which he so loved. Even in this he was, in a certain sense, associated with the person of Jesus. "The first who ought to have recognized Jesus Christ," Cardinal Giuseppe Siri said in 1972, "are those who sent him to the cross; the same thing happened as well to Padre Pio…. He was reduced to a reject, was secreted away, impeded, even to the point of being prohibited from communicating with the people."

For two years, from 1931 to 1933, he was in fact ordered not to have any contact with the faithful and to celebrate the Holy Mass only in private. But he accepted all this with a humility of heart and an obedience which was truly moving. "I am the son of holy obedience," Padre Pio liked to repeat.

It is certainly not easy today, in a climate profoundly marked by secularization, to fully understand the significance and the value of obedience. It is enough, however, to think how this principle belongs to the very dynamic of the Gospel itself.

To know and to love Jesus it is necessary to follow him, entrusting oneself completely to that reality, the Church, which "today" makes it possible to meet him really. Without obedience, each one places himself as the ultimate criterion, clinging as a matter of fact, more or less consciously, not to one's own freedom but to power, to that mentality, that culture which, from time to time, is most powerful in society.

The dynamic of the Gospel, instead, is that of obedience. The Madonna, for example, was humble, that is obedient, and a virgin; but it was possible for her to remain a virgin only because she was obedient ("Behold the handmaid of the Lord; be it done unto me according to your word," Lk 1:38). Jesus himself was obedient, obedient even unto death, to the Father's plan ("Son though he was, he learned obedience from what he suffered" becoming "the source of eternal salvation for all who obey him," Heb 5:8).

For the Christian people, two thousand years later, it is the same. Obedience to God's plans, abandonment to the will of God, as it is manifested through the persons, circumstances and situations of life, are "signs" of belonging, or better, of communion with that reality, the Church, which continues in history the merciful and salvific Presence of Jesus. That implies, at times, the fact that one might be called to acquiesce to orders that can seem inopportune and unjustified. What really counts, though — except, obviously, for cases regarding unlawful and immoral orders — is the love with which one obeys those who represent authority.

The value lies in "offering" to God the suffering which every mortification carries with it, an offering, as those who have gone through it can testify, if sincerely made never fails to produce its fruits. Padre Pio often used to remind his spiritual children: "Where there is no obedience, there is no virtue; where there is no virtue there is no good; where there is no good there is no love; where there is no love, God is not there; where God is not, there is no Paradise."

At the same time, however, to emphasize the value of obedience does not mean that from the historical point of view — always observing charity — one must never reveal the faults and demerits of the men of the Church, since, even these carry out the Providence of God who permits them and makes use of them to carry out His mysterious designs. In this regard, Pope Leo XIII taught toward the end of the last century: "The Church historian will be that much more efficacious in making [the Church's] divine origin known, to the extent that he is most loyal not to dissimulate those trials which the faults of its children, and at times even of its ministers, have forced this spouse of Christ to undergo."

"When I go along with my superior I go along with God"

The attitude which dominated the life of Padre Pio, confronted with the unclear manner in which representatives of the ecclesiastical authority may have conducted themselves, was that of a filial obedience which did not ask or require an explanation. For half a century, more than once his Father Superior had to enter his cell to read him some letter or document from the authorities that punished him with severe restrictions. Padre Pio would immediately rise to his feet, listen with head bowed and, in the end, exclaim: "Deo gratias!"

At the height of the widespread tension in August of 1923, provoked by the news of his hasty transfer from San Giovanni Rotondo, Padre Pio wrote: "As a devoted son of holy obedience… I will obey without opening my mouth." He declared himself to be obedient because "their voice is for me that of God whom I want to serve faithfully until death; and with His help, I will obey whatever command no matter how painful it may be in my misery." And to the friar who had communicated to him the decision, thereafter revoked, of his imminent transfer, he said: "Here I am at your disposition. Let us go at once. When I go along with my superior I go along with God."

Even when suspended from the ministry of

the confessional — following accusations that were shown to be false, calumnious and self-interested — in silence, albeit it in tears, he obeyed the crushing disposition of the authorities. To those who tried to get him to say something to justify himself publicly, Padre Pio always offered a decisive "No." He could have granted interviews, defined himself as one "persecuted," rebelled and even written a new catechism. With faith and humility he suffered the onslaughts of "evil," permitted by God, comforted with this phrase of one who was saddened by his awareness of the defeat of "good": "Let your soul not be disturbed by the sad spectacle of human injustice; even this, in the economy of things, has its value. And on it you will one day see rise the unfailing triumph of divine justice."

And if he sometimes wept, those tears were not for himself but for those souls who were deprived of his witness specifically by those — and he also wept for them — who should have supported and defended him.

The decisions of those in authority were never contested by him. The great scientist Enrico Medi, who knew him personally, summed up his comportment in these words: "When the Church asked of him the sacrifice of not celebrating Mass, he did not celebrate it; when it asked of him the sacrifice of remaining closed in silence, he remained closed in silence; when it asked him to speak, he spoke, to pray and he prayed, to celebrate and he celebrated; when it asked him to disappear, he disappeared."

Thus, after a first rehabilitation in 1933, even when confronted by successive harsh restrictions, even to the point of a religious financial inquest permitted by John XXIII, which in the '60's brought him anew so much sorrow, Padre Pio found the strength to affirm: "Sweet is the hand of the Church even when it persecutes, because it is the hand of a Mother."

His definitive "rehabilitation" would take place on January 30, 1964, when Pope Paul VI, through Cardinal Ottaviani, announced that Padre Pio had been restored to every freedom in his ministry.

Two of Yesterday's
"Miracles" for the People of Today.

Padre Pio Prayer Groups

"Let's do something. Let us roll up our sleeves. Let us be the first to answer the appeal launched by the Roman Pontiff." It was a discrete suggestion, involving the faithful to whom it was addressed who approached him in confession. It was just a "passing thought" which, being contagious, spread rapidly from San Giovanni Rotondo well beyond the confines of the Peninsula. And thus were born the "Prayer Groups," another of Padre Pio's many miracles which today, it is estimated, involve more than 500,000 people throughout the world.

From the very beginning of his pontificate, Pius XII, pointing to brotherhood in Jesus Christ and to the duty of mutual spiritual assistance, appealed to believers that they might come and pray together. His appeals to prayer in common, in groups, intensified when the dark and tragic clouds of the Second World War, which would make the times more difficult and the rapport among men more rancorous, appeared on the horizon.

They were appeals which Pius XII made several times. "We need strong and close-knit phalanxes of men and young boys who, remaining strictly united to Christ, at least once a month would receive the bread of life and bring others to follow their example" (February 17, 1942). A little more than a year later (March 13, 1943) with the imperative, "Let us not be afraid, but let us pray," Pius XII asked for the formation of groups of men and young boys who were practicing and praying Catholics.

Once the war was over, confronted by the squalid spectacle of a world divided into opposing blocs and the evident weakening of the Christian faith, the invitation of the pope became much more explicit: "What the Church most urgently needs are faithful and groups of faithful, of every condition who, free from slavery to human respect, would conform all their life and activity to the commandments of God and to the law of Christ" (March 8, 1952).

Padre Pio, who knew well the importance and the power of prayer, immediately took up the invitation of the pope and already beginning in 1947 the first groups, scattered here and there throughout Italy, began to form spontaneously. They initially were born to support one of his works, the Casa Sollievo della Sofferenza: "Never tire of praying," Padre Pio exhorted. "Prayer does violence to the heart of God and obtains the graces necessary. Without prayer our Casa Sollievo della Sofferenza is a little like a plant deprived of air and sun." Very soon, however, responding to the invitation of Pius XII, Padre Pio said: "Let us do something. Let us roll up our sleeves. Let us be the first to respond to this appeal of the Roman Pontiff."

A document from 1949 points to the activity of the "groups of the faithful who had made up their minds to pray together." "Once or twice a month they would get together, assist at the Holy Mass, approach the Holy Sacraments, and recite the Holy Rosary in common.... We would be very happy if these groups would multiply, if possible under the guidance of a priest." The essential goals that the groups set for themselves — the glory of God, the salvation of evil men, the sanctification of souls — correspond to the fundamental goals of prayer itself: adoration and praise, thanksgiving, propitiation, and reparation.

The essential recommendation, frequently repeated by Padre Pio himself was this: "If the local ecclesiastical authority does not approve of these groups, there is only one solution possible: obey immediately. The holy Church is our common Mother, to whom we owe the most absolute and devout obedience."

Thus overcoming even the initial diffidence of some bishops — who looked suspiciously on all this devotion to the friar of the stigmata — the prayer groups found an ever widening diffusion. Pope Paul VI, on September 24, 1975, spoke of "Padre Pio of Pietrelcina, who, among the many great and good things that he has accomplished, has given birth to this great company, almost a river, of persons who pray and who, following his example and in the hope of his spiritual assistance, dedicate themselves to the Christian life and give witness to their communion in prayer, acts of charity, poverty of spirit and in the dynamism that comes from their Christian profession."

"A river of persons who pray," that is what the prayer groups of Padre Pio were called when on May 3, 1986, with the signature of the then Cardinal Secretary of State, Agostino Casaroli, their Statutes were granted approval on the part of the Holy See. "In putting the new Statutes into effect" — Pope John Paul II had an opportunity to emphasize in 1988 — "the groups are now permitted to have a sure directive which guides the members in their spirituality and in their participation in the life of the parish and the diocese. Strictly united to the authentic Magisterium of the Church and the indications of their own bishop, the prayer groups can now better realize their personal formation in their liturgical and pastoral life and in the exercise of charity toward their neighbor." Today the prayer groups number nearly 1,600 in Italy and 400 abroad spread in 32 countries. The "miracle" continues.

The Casa Sollievo della Sofferenza

"On this night the great work of my earthly life begins." These words pronounced by Padre Pio on the night of January 9, 1940 are filled with audacity. It is the audacity that always accompanies the work of those who are touched by the grace of God. They were words spoken in confidence to a few friends which pointed to a project that some will define as "megalomania," but which was born of the urgency to respond to the immanent needs of the moment. A project that, without public contribution, but trusting solely on the intervention of divine Providence, would bring into being, in a zone totally deprived of structures of assistance, that which today, with a capacity of some 1200 beds, is one of the most modern and well equipped hospitals in the world: the Casa Sollievo della Sofferenza.

This "miracle" began on a winter night in 1940, almost as an outcome of the friendship between Padre Pio and three of his "spiritual children," who some time before had moved to San Giovanni Rotondo just in order to be closer to that extraordinary presence which had unexpectedly filled their lives with meaning. We are talking about Doctor Guglielmo Sanguinetti, a Tuscan doctor and ex-Mason, converted by Padre Pio; Doctor Carlo Kiswarday, a pharmacist who came from Zadar in Croatia, attracted by the stigmata of Padre Pio; and Doctor Mario Sanvico, a scientific agriculturist, who became a "spiritual son" of the friar of Pietrelcina.

The winter of 1940 was an especially harsh one for San Giovanni Rotondo, and not only for it. For several months in the rest of Europe the Nazi fury had unleashed the wretched and lacerating exploits of the Second World War. And Italy prepared to take her part, with the consequences we all know too well of death, mourning, suffering and sorrow.

It is in this context of misery and great uncertainty for the future that the idea of constructing a great hospital at the service of the sick poor matured in Padre Pio and in this little group of friends. Padre Pio placed in the hands of Doctor Kiswarday the first "brick," the first offering: a ten-franc gold piece given to him as a gift some days earlier by an unknown elderly lady. "On this night," he said, "the great work of my earthly life begins."

Actually Padre Pio had been thinking about this project for some time. The Lord through his hands had granted healing to several persons, but he was perfectly aware that this was only a matter of a few drops of goodness and mercy compared to the open sea of suffering humanity. "In every illness Jesus suffers," he said. "In every poor person who is sick Jesus suffers twice." And the area of the Gargano promontory, during the first decades of the nineteen hundreds, was a depressed zone in every respect, and not only in terms of sanitation and hygiene. Likewise depressed were several other zones in Italy, above all the mountainous areas and the open countrysides. Isolated for lack of roads and means of locomotion, it was difficult for those of the Gargano who were sick to reach the hospitals of Foggia or Naples.

As soon as he arrived at San Giovanni Rotondo, Padre Pio immediately understood the situation and he began to break through the solitude and abandonment in which the population lived. In January of 1925, in the quarters of a former convent of Poor Clare nuns, he established the first

clinic in which the poor could come to be cured free of charge. It was the civil hospital of St. Francis: two small corridors with twenty beds and adequate sanitary facilities. This attempt, however, was destined to come to an end. In fact, in 1938, an earthquake seriously damaged the structure.

St. Francis Hospital was, at any rate, a proving stage for the grand intuition which in 1940 began to take shape, trusting exclusively — the historical context under the circumstances would not have permitted anything else — on the help of Providence. Among the friends and devotees of Padre Pio there arose a veritable race to outdo one another in generosity. From France, devastated by the war, the first solid "stone" of the new construction arrived. A friend of his, Emanuele Brunatto, had been able to collect some three and a half million francs. For the most part, though, what added up were the little offerings of simple folk along with a few dollars which immigrants sent from America.

The work, in the meantime, went on steadily and never relied on loans from banks or institutions. When there was no more money, Padre Pio invited the workers to work "for charity." And so, as had happened centuries earlier with the great cathedrals of the Middle Ages, the construction of the hospital became a work of the people, involving even those who had never had any experience with mortar and bricks.

"Crazy megalomaniacs," was the way the supporters of the work were called, so impossible did it seem that one of the most modern and efficient hospital complexes could ever be built on that rocky and inhospitable outcropping. Even this "miracle" however would be realized in the end.

The Casa Sollievo della Sofferenza was finished in 1956, able to hold three hundred beds. To inaugurate it on May 5 was Cardinal Lercaro who said: "Where there is God, there is charity and love. Are you not aware of this in San Giovanni Rotondo? Yes, all the world is aware of the fact: God is here." And truly the news of what had happened in this little center of the Gargano spread rapidly: the *New York Times Magazine* defined the work in San Giovanni Rotondo as "a hospital complex among the most beautiful and modern in the world, fully equipped with every possible instrument." Pope Pius XII, speaking to a group of doctors, defined the Casa Sollievo della Sofferenza as "the fruit of one of the highest possible intuitions, of an ideal matured over time and perfected through contact with the most diverse and cruel aspects of moral and physical suffering in society."

But that was not enough. Padre Pio immediately set himself to expanding the hospital so that within the space of a few years the number of beds was doubled. The Casa Sollievo della Sofferenza was by now propelled toward a new goal. There were actually more than thirty functioning departments, some of which were "pilot" projects, in which provision was made for experimentation: from medical genetics to neurosurgery, from the study of diabetes to that of nuclear medicine. The time spent in the hospital by patients annually reached some 10,000 units and to provide for their assistance, in a building that held 1200 beds, there was a small army of 400 doctors and 1200 nurses.

The development of the Casa Sollievo della Sofferenza was prophetically outlined by Padre Pio in his discourse at the inauguration: "This work that you see here today," he said, "is at the beginning of its life, but in order for it to grow and to reach maturity, it must be nourished, and for this reason I call once again on your generosity so that it does not perish from lack of nourishment but will become a hospital city technically adequate for the most demanding clinical needs. A place of prayer and science where human beings can meet one another in Christ crucified as one fold under the one shepherd."

The Mass is ended

The death of Padre Pio

September 22, 1968. Thousands of the faithful literally invaded San Giovanni Rotondo. The Capuchin fathers had organized the festivities honoring the fifty years (1918-1968) of Padre Pio's stigmata. The day of the anniversary, September 20, fell on a Friday. So for convenience, in order to allow a greater participation on the part of the pilgrims, the solemn celebration was postponed until Sunday when an international gathering of the prayer groups and the ceremony of the blessing of the first stone of the monumental Via Crucis was scheduled. In reality, already on the evening of Thursday the 19th, the town was full of people. In the boarding houses and hotels there wasn't a single room available and many were constrained to spend the night in their automobiles and buses.

Padre Pio is very old. He is now 81. In these last days his health had been declining rapidly. To the blood which dripped from his wounds, to his mysterious high fever, were added a bronchial asthma which made his breathing labored and a dizziness which confined him to bed for days at a time, and kept him from celebrating Mass. In 1967, at age 80, he was persuaded to use a wheelchair to go from one place to another in the monastery.

The day of his anniversary, Friday, was spent as usual. Padre Pio celebrated Mass at 5:00 in the morning in order then to dedicate himself to the confessional and to prayer. In the evening there was a huge procession which ended with a display of fireworks as a finale. From the center of town, a crowd of devotees, led by the Mayor, joyfully marched with torches in hand up to the plaza in front of the church. The pilgrims remained there for a long time in prayer under the windows of the monastery hoping that Padre Pio might appear and greet them.

Their waiting was in vain. Padre Pio did not take part in the festivities, a little perhaps because he was not pleased that a mystical phenomenon be celebrated with such clamor, and a little because he felt his own strength was ebbing away. That evening, in fact, he went to bed earlier than usual, even though he slept very little. It was an agitated night on account of his asthma, so much so that the doctor was urgently called. At a certain point it seemed that one attack stronger than the others would cut off his breathing.

At dawn on Saturday, he was not able to get up to celebrate his usual Mass at 5:00. Only in the afternoon did he manage to sit up in his wheel-chair and be taken into the packed church. He assisted at the Vespers of the Blessed Virgin and at the end blessed the crowd who thought they saw in his face signs of exhaustion.

And so Sunday arrived, the day of the big feast. During the night his asthma gave him some respite and so Padre Pio was able to rest. At 4:30 he therefore went down as usual into the sacristy to get ready to celebrate Mass at 5:00. There was a long wait, the church was full of pilgrims who never would have imagined that they would be attending the last Mass of Padre Pio. Since it was a feast day the Father Superior had arranged for the Mass to be sung. For the celebrant this meant notable fatigue. When he received communion, Padre Pio looked around himself, lost, saying: "And if I don't make it?" But those were the orders of the Superior and even this time, right to the end, he obeyed.

For Padre Pio, however, this required superhuman strength. Some photographs show his confused expression. In some of the recordings made at the time his voice can be heard labored and trembling. At the Preface, Padre Pio was so exhausted that he was not able to sing and so he recited it. When, not being able to hold back the tears, he pronounced the words of dismissal "The Mass is ended. Go in peace!" the crowd could not stop applauding and crying out "Evviva!" These acclamations contributed to disorienting the Padre, who in fact, as he was preparing to descend the steps of the altar, collapsed. He would have fallen to the floor had his assistants not promptly held him up and put him in his wheelchair. He only had the strength to repeat over and over, "My children, my children!"

Taken back to his cell, at 10:30 he wanted once again to go to the window facing the choir of the old church — where fifty years earlier he had received the stigmata — to greet and bless the festive crowd. During the day the crypt carved out of stone under the presbytery of the big church and the first stone of the monumental Via Crucis were also blessed.

During the night between the 22nd and the 23rd of September, Padre Pio wanted at his side Padre Pellegrino da Sant'Elia a Pianisi. Like a fearful little child, he asked Padre Pellegrino to keep him company. "At one point," Padre Pellegrino recalls, "he took my hands into his own and squeezed them tightly. He trembled like a baby. Every few minutes he asked me the time, as if he had an important appointment that he could not miss." Padre Pio felt that by now the end was near. It was just a little past midnight when he asked: "Have you said Mass yet?" "No." "Then say it for me in the morning." He made his last confession, renewed the vows of his religious profession and implored Padre Pellegrino to ask forgiveness — for him — of his confreres for the annoyance he had caused and to ask his confreres and his spiritual children to pray for his soul.

Around 1:00, he got up from his bed and went out on the terrace to look at the stars. He stayed there for about five minutes, then went back into his cell, and sat in an easy chair. His face became whiter and whiter, and his forehead broke out in a cold sweat. His lips becoming blue barely moved while repeating over and over again, "Jesus! Mary!" Padre Pellegrino started to go call for help. "Don't wake anyone up," Padre Pio suggested. It was about 2:30 on the 23rd of September when Padre Pio breathed his last. "Jesus! Mary!" were his last words.

The disappearance of the stigmata

According to some witnesses Padre Pio knew the exact day of his death. When, in 1918, he received the stigmata, Jesus spoke a phrase which he never referred to his spiritual director, but which he confided to some of his spiritual children. Finding himself with bleeding wounds, Padre Pio turned to Jesus imploring him to take these signs away from him. "Make me suffer, make me die of suffering," he had asked in his prayer, "but take away these signs which fill me with such profound confusion." Jesus answered him: "You will bear them for fifty years and then you will come to me."

After exactly fifty years the stigmata disappeared and Padre Pio was taken into heaven to Jesus.

At the moment of his death, in fact, the signs of the stigmata completely disappeared from the body of Padre Pio. Not only were the wounds closed but the complete absence of any form of scar was also verified. In their place, on the hands, feet and side, there was new flesh, regenerated (recreated?) rosy in color, like that of a baby. The process of the disappearance of the stigmata had probably begun two years before his death. The first to shrink were those of his feet and side. During the celebration of his last Mass, on September 22, 1968, the stigmata were still visible on the palm of his left hand. In less than twenty four hours even this completely disappeared without leaving any trace or scar.

This fact left the Capuchin friars disconcerted, at least initially, and so they kept silent about this detail in order not to create any scandal or disorientation among the faithful. The "mystery" willed to accompany Padre Pio until the end of his existence. What explanation could be given, what meaning could be attributed to this last phenomenon for which, once again, no scientific explanation can be found?

Padre Gerardo Di Flumeri, Vice Postulator of the Cause of his Beatification, offers a theological explanation. The mystery of the Cross, he affirms, is essentially the paschal mystery, that is, the mystery of the death and resurrection of Jesus. In this sense, besides the signs of the passion, God willed to renew in Padre Pio of Pietrelcina also the mystery of the resurrection of Christ. The disappearance of the stigmata from the body of Padre Pio, explains Padre Gerardo Di Flumeri, "appears to us to be the sign manifesting that God has been pleased to accept his long and bitter sacrifice, and has given to him, the first stigmatized priest, a glorified recompense by means of this beginning of the resurrection of the flesh."

DEVOTIONS

ON THE WAY TO SAINTHOOD

A saint of modern times

"A saint of modern times, once again manifesting all the power of the Risen Christ, who with His Holy Spirit is always renewing the face of the earth." It is the morning of May 5, 1996. At San Giovanni Rotondo the celebration of the fortieth anniversary of the foundation of the Casa Sollievo della Sofferenza is underway, and Cardinal Angelo Sodano, who had come to the Gargano for this purpose, describes the figure of the Servant of God, Padre Pio of Pietrelcina, in these words.

"A saint of modern times": these words of the Vatican Secretary of State are indicative. For several years, also on account of the excesses and the fanaticism which had at times sprung up around his person, Padre Pio was not looked upon very favorably by some men in the Church. The then Congregation of the Holy Office had imposed on him the most severe restrictions, which Padre Pio kept in an exemplary way. But a lot of time has

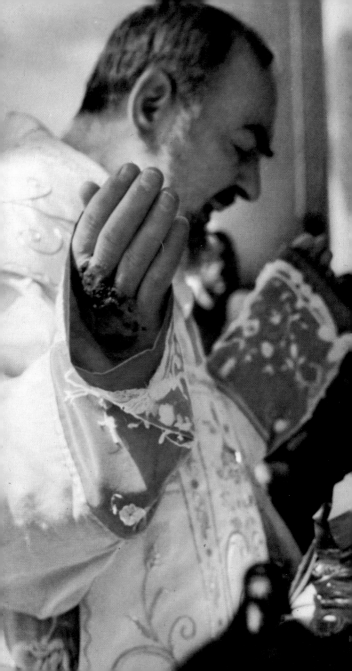

passed, and the time now supports the goodness of his charisms. The misunderstandings having been cleared up and everything having been carefully sorted out, Padre Pio is now thus defined by an authoritative member of the hierarchy as "a saint of modern times" or even as "a giant of sanctity."

In fact Cardinal Sodano went on to say in his discourse: "In this century of so many conflicts, of so many confrontations, in a century of so many fratricidal wars and rampant egoism, God has raised up in the Italian Church, in this noble land of the Puglia, a giant of sanctity, to call the men of today back to their vocations as creatures of God and as children of the same Father who is in heaven."

These words of Cardinal Sodano, above all, are words which allow the many — and there are millions in every part of the world — to hope, waiting for the day when they will see Padre Pio raised to the honors of the altar as early as possible. The most numerous voices raised in prayer and affection have, in fact, come from the people. If Padre Pio during the fifty years of his stigmata had brought such attention from so many (even non-believers) to himself and to his works, such attention certainly did not cease with his death. And thus even the polemics which accompanied him in life were transformed into an even more intense veneration.

The immense and moving assembly of th
more than 100,000 people who on September 2€
1968 invaded the very confines of San Giovann
Rotondo were literally multiplied with the passin
of time. It is enough to think that every year, ac
cording to some estimates, from four to five mil
lion pilgrims arrive at the little center of th
Gargano.

The greatest proof of his virtue, in fact, i
given by the people of today, with their remem
brance of his life, their pilgrimages to the place
dear to him, their remaining in prayer before hi
tomb, their recourse to his intercession. And the
are not few in number among the Christian peopl
who — without any kind of fanaticism — than
him for some healing or grace obtained from Goc
by means of prayer addressed to His Servant.

Here we are not dealing with secondary mat
ters. To the Church it is not sufficient to recogniz
that a Servant of God had practiced in life the Chris
tian virtues to an heroic degree. To officially pro
claim a person a "saint" or even only as "blessed
an ultimate "seal" is required. Treating an argumen
that has to do with the hereafter, the Church re
quires that human judgment be in some wa
confirmed by God with an explicit sign. A miracl
is necessary. And it must be a miracle obtainec
through the intercession of the candidate for beati
fication or canonization and it must take place af

ter his or her death. In this case, those which were attributed to the person in life have no value.

Every day at San Giovanni Rotondo miracles by the dozen, even among the most extraordinary, are claimed. Every case is catalogued, but only the most clear cut, the most humanly unexplainable, are taken into consideration and studied with requests for further documentation, medical proofs and testimonies.

The term "miracle" today bothers a certain type of mentality that would like to reduce Christianity to a series of moral "rules" acceptable to modern man. The saints, instead, are there to witness that the source of all moral conduct is the "miracle" of the grace of God. For this reason the Church never tires of requiring the "miracle" as a proof of sanctity.

In the long and delicate journey that leads to an official declaration of sanctity, Padre Pio has already completed a good part of the way. One year and two months after his death, on November 23, 1969, Bishop Antonio Cunial, Apostolic Administrator of Manfredonia, ordered the initiation of the preliminary inquiry by gathering up his writings and the testimonies necessary before any eventual opening of the process of beatification and canonization could begin. On May 3, 1972 an entire national episcopal conference, Poland's, with a letter signed by two cardinals and forty-three archbishops and bishops, sent to Pope Paul VI the first request to introduce the process of beatification, a process that, after receiving the "nulla osta" of the Holy See, was officially opened on March 20, 1983.

In the span of seven years, during the "gathering of information" phase, the depositions of more than seventy witnesses were reconstructed, verified and compared. All the documentation was collected in twenty-three volumes to which an additional twenty volumes containing the writings of Padre Pio were appended. The material was sent to the Vatican Congregation for the Causes of Saints in 1990, which at the end of a long, stringent and complex examination presented a detailed report to the Pope, from whom final word was awaited. On December 18, 1997, in the Sala del Consistorio in the Vatican, Pope John Paul II confirmed the heroic virtues of the Servant of God, Padre Pio, and conferred on him the title of Venerable. Another milestone took place at a meeting with members of the Congregation for the Causes of Saints on December 21, 1998 when the needed "miracle" for the next step was approved, and the date of May 2, 1999 was set for his Beatification.

PLACES MADE FAMOUS BY PADRE PIO'S PRESENCE

Pietrelcina

"I did a lot for San Giovanni Rotondo while I was alive, but I will do even more for Pietrelcina after I have died." Thus spoke Padre Pio of the city of his birth, May 25, 1887. And in effect even this "prophecy" of the good Padre is being fulfilled. In fact, tens of thousands of pilgrims each year arrive in this little center in the Province of Benevento to visit the places of Padre Pio's infancy and youth.

Apart from the most important liturgical feasts, solemn celebrations are organized on May 5 to celebrate Padre Pio's feast day, on May 25, his birthday, and on May 26, the day of his baptism. At Pietrelcina everything speaks of Padre Pio: from the humble home where he was born, to the tiny church of Sant'Anna where he was baptized, to the road which he used to walk reciting the rosary, to the house in the country owned by the Forgione family, to the Piana Romana, where under an elm tree he received the first stigmata which then disappeared only to reappear later in 1918 in a visible way and remain with him until his death.

San Giovanni Rotondo

It is impossible to establish how many pilgrims each year arrive at this town situated in the mountains of the Gargano in the Province of Foggia and made famous throughout the world by the Friar of the Stigmata. According to some, four to five million have been registered to date. Dizzying esteem, but in some way understandable, if one considers that every year the Capuchin Fathers distribute around 750,000 hosts for Holy Communion. An extraordinary influx that becomes almost unmanageable on the dates dear to the spiritual children of Padre Pio: Holy Week, his feast day and birthday in May, the month of September with its remembrance of his reception of the stigmata and his death; and also, the feast of the Madonna delle Grazie patroness of the town, the feast of the Founder of the Order, St. Francis, as well as all the other collateral manifestations organized by the city officials and by the Casa Sollievo della Sofferenza.

Precisely in order to be able to meet the ever increasing needs of the faithful, the Capuchin Fathers in 1994 began the construction of a new church which was to rise just south of the monastery and extend toward the valley, ideally following the line of sight of Padre Pio when he looked out of the window of his cell each morning. The building, in the form of a shell, designed by Renzo

Piano, architect of world fame, will accommodate up to ten thousand persons.

The monastery and the old church

The first Capuchin Fathers arrived at San Giovanni Rotondo in 1540 and set to work at once on the construction of the actual monastery with the blessing of the then Archbishop of Siponto, Cardinal Giovanni Maria Ciocchi del Monte, who afterwards became pope taking the name of Julius III. Next to the monastery, on July 5, 1676, the little church dedicated to Santa Maria delle Grazie was consecrated with great solemnity. With the suppression of the Religious Orders in 1866 the monastery was reduced to a miserable state and the little church often served as a refuge for goats. In 1867 the communal administration considered selling the building and the land belonging to it in order to build, with the receipts, a hospital. The sale however, did not go through and in 1908 the friars once again came into possession of the monastery. On July 28, 1916 for the first time a young friar by the name of Padre Pio of Pietrelcina arrived.

The church possesses a gracious lunette depicting the Virgin with Child, St. Francis and St. Michael the Archangel. Inside there is an altar dedicated to St. Francis, on which for more than twenty years, from 1935 to 1959, Padre Pio celebrated the

Holy Sacrifice of the Mass. One can also see the confessional where Padre Pio from 1935 to the day of his death heard the confessions of women. The men's confessional is, instead, in the sacristy. On the high altar there is the miraculous image of the Madonna delle Grazie, protectress of San Giovanni Rotondo.

The ancient choir of the stigmata

This little choir, situated above the front door of the little church and dominated by a crucifix, is the one witness, on September 20th, 1918, of the extraordinary event of the stigmatization. But it is also witness to the long and impassioned prayer of Padre Pio to Jesus and to the "Madonnina" delle Grazie. From here at noon Padre Pio would lead the Marian prayer of the Angelus with the faithful gathered in the little church.

The "little room" of St. Francis

This is the place where the faithful normally would congregate who were waiting for Padre Pio to pass in order to ask him for some material or spiritual aid or simply to kiss his hand. On the part of Padre Pio: a brief bit of banter, some advice, an occasional unexpected gesture and a blessing.

His cell

It has the famous number "1" of the monastery of Santa Maria delle Grazie. Here, in a few square feet, Padre Pio prayed, suffered and spent his rare moments of repose. Here also his life ended and from here he went to the house of the Father. The Capuchin Fathers have maintained it intact just as Padre Pio left it on the day of his death. In it one can notice, among other things: a little table on which are placed some fingerless gloves with which he covered the stigmata and a small rag for the wound in his side; a kneeler and a handkerchief which he used to bless the pilgrims from his window; a little bed and wash basin; on a shelf the slippers worn up to the last hour of his life; the armed chair, where he used to sit to prepare for Holy Mass, hear the pains and joys of his spiritual children and from which he would depart for Paradise.

The big church, the crypt and his tomb

In order to deal with the continual and extraordinary influx of pilgrims it was necessary to construct, alongside the old church, a new and more spacious one, which was inaugurated on July 1st of 1959. Nine years later the crypt carved under the high altar was blessed. Padre Pio died on the following day, at 2:30 in the morning of September 23, 1968, with the rosary in his hand and "Jesus!... Mary!" on his lips. His body lies there, in the crypt, protected by a monolithic block of Labrador granite weighing 1300 pounds. The burial of his mortal remains took place on the evening of September 26 at 10:30. On May 23, 1987, Pope John Paul II, during his pastoral visit to San Giovanni Rotondo, stopped to pray before his tomb.

The Via Crucis

A place of prayer and summit of any pilgrimage, the monumental Way of the Cross, realized by the celebrated sculptor Francesco Messina, rises alongside the Capuchin monastery on the enchanting and scenic hill above the church of Santa Maria delle Grazie. Inaugurated on May 25, 1971, Padre Pio was not able to see it finished, but he was in time, on the day before he died, to bless the laying of the first stone. In the spot where he stopped for this ceremony, a bronze statue of Padre Pio has been erected, over two meters (or nearly seven feet) high. An eloquent detail can be found at the fifth station: the Cyrenian carrying the cross in Jesus' place has the face of Padre Pio.

The author of the work, Francesco Messina, is one of Padre Pio's great converts, so much so that, in recalling the day when he first met him, he wrote: "I was 'born' on April 1, 1949."

PRAYERS

Prayer to obtain graces and the glorification of Blessed Padre Pio of Pietrelcina

O Jesus, full of grace and love, victim for sinners, who, driven by love for our souls, willed to die on the cross, I humbly pray that You might glorify, even on this earth, Blessed Padre Pio of Pietrelcina who, in his generous participation in Your suffering, loved You so and spent himself for the glory of Your Father and for the good of souls.

I implore You, therefore, to want to grant me, through his intercession, the grace (*indicate here the grace sought*) which I so ardently desire.

Three *Glory Be*'s.

The Coroncina to the Sacred Heart of Jesus

The coroncina to the Sacred Heart of Jesus was recited every day by Padre Pio for all those who had asked him for his prayers. The faithful, who were also asked to recite it each day, would in this way unite themselves spiritually to the prayer of their venerated Padre.

I. — O my Jesus, who said, "Truly I say to you, ask and you shall receive, seek and you shall find, knock and it will be opened to you!", behold I knock, I seek, I ask for the grace....

Our Father, Hail Mary, Glory Be
Sacred Heart of Jesus, I trust and hope in You.

II. — O my Jesus, who said, "Truly I say to ou, whoever asks the Father anything in my name, e will be given it!", behold, in Your name, I ask he Father for the grace....

Our Father, Hail Mary, Glory Be
Sacred Heart of Jesus, I trust and hope in You.

III. — O my Jesus, who said, "Truly I say to ou, heaven and earth will pass away, but my vords will never pass away!", behold, relying on he infallibility of Your holy words, I ask for the race....

Our Father, Hail Mary, Glory Be
Sacred Heart of Jesus, I trust and hope in You.

O Sacred Heart of Jesus, to whom it is impos- ible not to have compassion on the unfortunate, ave pity on us poor sinners, and grant the graces vhich we ask of You through the Immaculate Heart f Mary, Your most tender Mother and ours.

St. Joseph, foster father of the Sacred Heart f Jesus, pray for us.

Salve Regina.

Prayer to Jesus

Jesus lives who, notwithstanding my every fault, wants to make me a sharer in his sorrows. O how insupportable sorrow is when suffered far from the cross. But how sweet it becomes if one suffers close to the cross of Jesus. Everything becomes easy for the soul, even when it feels itself oppressed and intoxicated by every sort of grief. And were there not in the depths of this soul that holy fear of being able to displease the divine spouse, it would feel itself to be in Paradise. The soul placed in such a state, as often as it turns to the Divine Master, says to him, "Yes, O Jesus, your yoke is easy and your burden is light." It pleases God to hear from every soul this new way of suffering.

Prayer to the Virgin Mary

I salute you, Holy Mother, abyss of grace and purity, unsurpassable masterpiece of the Creator, tabernacle of the Most High, depository of the divine secrets, woman clothed in light, enchanting dove, most pure light who renews creation through him whom you carried in your womb like the dew of a rose, the first step on our path to salvation; morning star, sure guide of humanity toward the divine sun, Jesus.

This book was designed and published by St. Pauls/ Alba House, the publishing arm of the Society of St. Paul, an international religious congregation of priests and brothers dedicated to serving the Church through the communications media. For information regarding this and associated ministries of the Pauline Family of Congregations, write to the Vocation Director, Society of St. Paul, 7050 Pinehurst, Dearborn, Michigan 48126 or check our internet site, www.albahouse.org